Good Citizenship Online

UNDERSTANDING CITIZENSHIP

Leonard Clasky

CiViCS FOR THE REAL WORLD™

Rosen Classroom™

Published in 2019 by The Rosen Publishing Group, Inc.
29 East 21st Street, New York, NY 10010

Book Design: Rachel Rising
Editor: Ryan Wolf

Photo Credits: Cover AVAVA/Shutterstock.com; pp. 4, 14 Monkey Business Images/Shutterstock/com; p. 7 ESB Professional/Shutterstock.com; p. 8 goodluz/Shutterstock.com; p. 11 stockfour/Shutterstock.com; p. 12 Tyler Olson/Shutterstock.com.

ISBN: 9781538365519
6-pack ISBN: 9781538365526

Manufactured in the United States of America

CPSIA Compliance Information: Batch #WS18RC: For Further Information contact Rosen Publishing, New York, New York at 1-800-237-9932

Table of Contents

Young Citizens Online

It's important to be a good citizen in real life. This means you're aware of your rights and **responsibilities**. You try to work for the common good. That means you do things that benefit your community.

It's important to be a good citizen online, too. This means you act in a way that's safe, respectful, and careful.

Rules and Responsibilities

Your parents may have rules for what you do on the computer and when or if you can go online. There may be rules for using computers at school, too. It's important to follow these rules. This is one of your responsibilities. The rules are there to make sure you're safe and other people can use the computers, too.

Ask an Adult

Your parents and teachers will likely have rules about what websites you can visit. Listen to them!

You can find lots of good **information** online, but some websites are unsafe. Always ask an adult before you visit a new website. Tell them if the website asks you for any information. You should also tell an adult if anything makes you feel uncomfortable online.

Privacy Is Important

Some of your information is private. You shouldn't give it to someone just because they ask.

Never tell anyone online your real name, your age, or your address. Don't share pictures of yourself! Don't share this information about your friends or family members either. If a website needs a password, talk to your parents or teacher about setting up a good one.

Respect!

Part of being a good citizen online is showing respect for other people. This doesn't mean talking to anyone who asks! You can always say no. But when you do **communicate** online, you should be kind. Don't bully people online. It's not OK just because it isn't in person. You might think people don't know who you are. But there are always ways of knowing!

Learning and Growing

As you get older, you'll be able to do more online. You might be able to get **social media** accounts or visit different websites. It will be important to learn how to judge information. Sometimes you can trust information. Sometimes you can't! Good online citizens learn how to tell the difference.

Glossary

communicate: To share knowledge or feelings.

information: Facts about a subject.

responsibility: Something someone trusts you to do.

social media: Websites through which people can talk to and share with other people.

Index